WHISTLING THORN

11/21

Scholastic Children's Books,
Scholastic Publications Ltd,
7-9 Pratt Street, London NW1 OAE, UK

Scholastic Inc.,
555 Broadway, New York, NY 10012, USA

Scholastic Canada Ltd,
123 Newkirk Road, Richmond Hill,
Ontario, Canada L4C 3G5

Ashton Scholastic Pty Ltd,
PO Box 579, Gosford, New South Wales,
Australia

Ashton Scholastic Ltd,
Private Bag 92801, Penrose, Auckland,
New Zealand

First published in hardback by Scholastic Publications Ltd, 1993
This edition published 1994

Copyright © Helen Cowcher, 1993

ISBN: 0 590 55422 0

Typeset by Rapid Reprographics
Printed and bound in Hong Kong by the Paramount Printing Group Company

WHISTLING THORN

HELEN COWCHER

Hippo

Long ago, on the grasslands of Africa,
there grew acacia bushes.
They were the favourite food
of giraffes and rhinos.

Giraffe stretched out his long tongue
and grasped the juicy rich leaves.
Rhino nibbled contentedly.
The bushes were many...

...but so, in those far off days,
were the giraffes and rhinos.
Even the tiniest acacia buds were eaten.

Rhino, like all his fellow rhinos,
rested for hours in the shade,
each day,

and only wandered to the acacias
when he felt very hungry.
The rhinos never ate at any bush
long enough to do real harm.

But the giraffes ate constantly.
They could reach even the highest branches,
taking far too much from each bush.

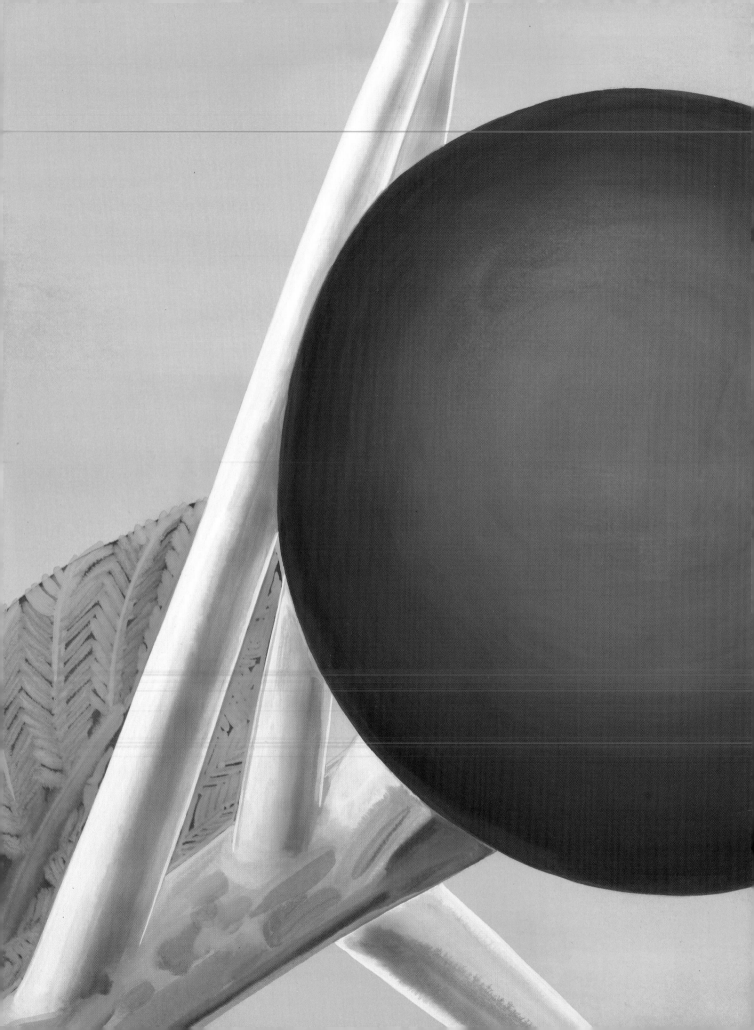

As time passed, the acacias grew
sharp thorns, some shaped like galls.
Ants smelled sweet acacia nectar
and came to make their nests.

They made entrance holes in the galls.
The wind came blowing across the savannah
and piped through the holes
like the music of a thousand flutes.

The sound of WHISTLING THORNS!

One day, a hungry giraffe
was tugging at the acacia shoots,
relentlessly shaking the thorny branches.

He rocked the gall homes!
Frenzied ants scrambled out,

crawling in a steady stream
all over the giraffe's muzzle,
stinging as they went.

They climbed around the giraffe's eye...

... irritating him so much that
he could stand it no longer.
He moved on,
shaking the ants free.

The same fate awaited each giraffe;
one by one, spurred on
by stinging ants,
they moved quickly to other
whistling thorn bushes.

Now the bushes had time to grow fresh leaves,
while the giraffes and rhinos could still
eat their favourite food.
A warm breeze washed over them
as they grazed under the
hot savannah sun and flute music
flowed from the whistling thorns.